FACE · TO · FA

MICHELLE AKERS

WITH JUDITH A. NELSON

SUCCESS^{SM} FACTORS

FACE TO FACE
WITH MICHELLE AKERS

by Michelle Akers with Judith A. Nelson

Published by:
Success Factors
c/o Integrated Resources
100 Sunport Lane
Orlando, FL 32809
1-800-729-4351

ISBN Number: 1-57902-049-6
Integrated Resources Product Number: 1536e

First Printing, November 1996
Second Printing, March 1997
Third Printing, July 1997

Cover photo: Umbro and Walter Iooss, Jr.
Back cover photos: Brett Whitesell and Tom Quinn

Cover design by: Journey Communications

SUCCESS ᔆᔉ
FACTORS

Foreword

I was first confronted by this scrawny, curly headed waif of 15 during her freshman year in high school. We formed a quick bond with each other through our love of soccer. I quickly found that Michelle was in "deep weeds" personally and emotionally. I took an interest in her and responded to her cry for help. This was the beginning of a long friendship as teacher, coach, counselor and confidant.

Michelle's story is a wonderful testimony of a young lady who braved all odds and continued to confront the challenges she faced. Her stubbornness, determination, faith, and finally, her understanding of God's grace will prove to be an inspiration to young people who are facing adversity in their lives.

I strongly recommend this book to anyone who is struggling with who they are and is trying to make sense out of life. There is purpose, direction and hope as Michelle clearly lays out a powerful message for her readers.

Al Kovats

Redmond, Washington

Acknowledgments

This is my first book, and therefore, the first drop of reality that has been an off-hand joke or afterthought for many years. I have laughed, celebrated, marveled, and many times, staggered through my life with the thought that one particular experience or another would make a great story someday. And now look! This thing is a reality. And only a reality because many others believed in it and me besides myself. This book about my life has become a book about many lives and the many people who have shaped, contributed, and even knocked me down over my lifetime. It is because of them that I am who I am and have achieved the platform to share my experiences with you.

I have to say the first time I read *Face to Face* cover to cover, I was a little anxious about making it public. After all, I am spilling my guts and declaring the hurts and trauma of my life to the world. Something to think twice about for sure! Also, my dad (who is right 99.5 percent of the time) thinks this book is too one sided and does not convey the full picture of who Michelle Akers is and what my life encompasses. He is right in that respect. There is more to me than what is between these pages. However, I chose to ignore his latest advice because many of the most difficult and painful moments in my life have turned into some of the most precious and powerful. Difficulty and challenge are the surest and most poignant means to grow and learn. It is my hope to convey that philosophy to you too.

So, look out. This book is intense. It is sad. It is full of struggle and tough times. And it seems almost as if I have labored or trudged through my life without happiness and joy. Not so. Admittedly, I have been "through the mill" more than once, but my life has also been full of achievement, laughter and celebration.

I have chosen to highlight some of my toughest moments in order to communicate a very important and pointed message: to help you see that even world champions and gold medalists cry, get sick, and want to give up at times. That life is hard, but there is a power beyond the difficulties of life. My hope is that you will understand how and why I have been able to overcome . . . and even more importantly, that you can do it too.

Now, to thank the million people who have been part of this book and part of who I am. High fives to the following:

My heartfelt thanks to those who jump started and put together this project: Judy and Steve Douglass, Judy (Judith) Nelson, and Campus Crusade for Christ. You guys are studs. To Mike Kos, I can juggle over 100 now. To Kovats, one high school teacher who made a world and an eternal difference. Thanks for showing me the Way. To Goz, Hades, and Special K, guys, can you believe this?! Special thanks to Northland Community Church and my fave preacher man and wife, the Hunters, who by living their lives inspired me to take my toe off the ground in deep water. You rock! To Stevie, who has been my pillar of strength through some very tough times. A big hug and smack on the head to you. Dude, I love you. You're the greatest (and don't let it go to your head). To my team(s), teammates, coaches, PTs, and docs over the years. GO USA! And thanks for the glue, tape, stitches, laughter and fun. GOLD MEDAL, baby!

To my family who has followed and cheered me across the globe, loved me when I was a jerk, made me eat my spinach and peas, and gave me the foundation, confidence and solace to achieve my dreams—I love you. P.S. Don't cry.

And lastly, I lay down my achievements, my person, my life to Christ. Dear Lord, it's me again. Thank you for this opportunity, the friends and family that surround me, and the peace, power and strength to go where you want and to become the person only you can make me.

Love,

Contents

Appendices

Chapter 1

World Champions!

The bus ride seemed to last an eternity. We sat in our white uniforms, cleats in hand and headphones blasting, waiting. Most players like to listen to something to get them pumped up, but I like calming music. No rock. Nothing raging. Something relaxing. To be steady. We were waiting to arrive at Tianhe Stadium in Gangzhou China, where we would play Norway in the 1991 inaugural women's World Cup final. As we drove, I looked out the window at the city and anticipated 9 p.m., when we would know the outcome of the championship. I wished I could fast-forward time to get a glimpse ahead and calm my nerves.

As always, when we walk out for the anthem, I looked for my dad. No matter how many people are in the stands—it could be 65,000 like at that final—I can always spot him. His wild blond hair and 6'3" frame didn't hinder this search—especially in contrast to the smaller and dark-headed Chinese. I finally located him and gave him the thumbs up.

Then the anthem began. It brought tears to my eyes and hit me like a wave. I realized, *This is it.* The anticipation of victory or defeat was almost too much for me. Then soccer legend and my idol, Pele, was introduced to each team. He shook hands with each player, offering a word of encouragement. I wondered how he felt before his first World Championship. He greeted me by name since we had met a few months earlier as spokespersons for Umbro.

After Pele's words of encouragement on the field, the game finally began. The Norwegians came out fired up. From the beginning, we had to withstand long driven balls, hard tackles and fierce attacks. They had come to play. But so had we. Twenty minutes into the game, we were awarded a free kick outside the goal box. My teammate Shannon Higgins and I stepped up to the ball, and after discussion, decided she'd take the kick. She lofted the ball into the six-yard box, where I jumped up and headed it past the defender and goalkeeper for a goal. We celebrated like maniacs. Unfortunately our lead was short-lived—they scored off a similar play just eight minutes later, making it 1-1 at half.

We walked off the field to chaos in the locker room. Coach Anson Dorrance and a couple of the players were yelling. Who should mark up? What kind of changes should we make? Everyone was really on edge. I just remember sitting there. Not listening to any of it, just wanting to go back out and play. As we walked through the tunnel back on to the field, goalkeeper coach Tony DiCicco walked beside me and said, "Mich, you're going to be the one. You're the one who is going to have to take control of this game." I nodded my head, "Okay. Okay, Tony." Then I just went out and played as hard as I could. I never doubted that we were going to win. Never doubted.

The second half was much the same, with the Norwegians banging long balls into our half, and our backs trying to clear it out. Many thought overtime or penalty kicks were inevitable, but I was confident we would get another one.

Then, our chance came. Shannon Higgins hit a long ball up field. The defender miskicked the ball back to her goalkeeper, and I intercepted it. The open net stood in front of me. I planted with my left leg, but I was so tired I almost fell over trying to stop myself. I passed it in with my right foot.

Later, people told me I caused them coronaries because I took so long to shoot the ball. After beating the keeper, I was at such a bad angle I had to make sure it would go in. I took my time. The only thought in my head was: Don't miss it! I put my fist in the air and shouted a loud "YES!" But I was so exhausted, my celebration was subdued. During the last 15 minutes of the game, we just tried to clear the ball out of the stadium.

Finally, the whistle blew. I looked at the ref to make sure it wasn't a foul, almost too afraid to hope the game was finally over. We celebrated just as I had imagined. We cried. We hugged. We yelled. We were in a frenzy running back and forth, not knowing where to go or whom to hug or what to say. It was awesome! Even now, it is all a blur.

Lining up for our medals, I looked out into the crowd. My dad stood out among the Chinese fans. He waved his arms wildly to get my attention. He was so proud. I realized all the parents, relatives and friends were as much a part of this World Cup team as any player or coach. They are the ones who hosed us down after muddy games, drove us to practice day after day and spent fortunes to send us to select camps, buying shoes and supporting us after college when we had no jobs. I waved back to Dad and the U.S. crowd just as frantically.

After the medal ceremony and banquet—where I received the Golden Boot Award for most goals in the tournament (I had 10 in six games)—our team and all the U.S. families, friends and fans danced, drank champagne and cheered throughout the night. The next morning we packed our medals and cleats and hopped on the train to Hong Kong, where we stuffed our faces with much-missed McDonald's food, and then embarked on the long trip home.

On the last leg from China, an elderly American lady next to me on the plane asked where I had been. I told her I was representing my country at the first women's World Cup of soccer.

"How'd you do?" she asked.

"We won," I replied proudly.

"That's nice," she said.

That was about the response we received from all of America. At JFK Airport in New York, there were four people awaiting our world championship team: an American journalist, a foreign journalist, then U.S. men's coach Bora Multinovic and a friend of mine. The team was disappointed. We had collected foreign papers en route back home heralding our success with big photos and long articles, so this lack of recognition really stung. It was like the rest of the world stopped and stared for one long moment, but the United States only blinked.

Each player received about $1,200 in bonus money; that didn't even cover my family's airfare to come see me play.

But it was still worth it. I think back to our arrival in China on November 12, 1991. Preparing for our first match against Sweden, we were giddy with excitement. I remember the set jaw and fierce determination in our eyes as we set out to beat Germany in the semifinals. I can still see our incredible U.S. fans and families cheering wildly, chanting "U.S.A." and waiting patiently outside the stadium after games.

It is amazing to think how far we have come. We began only seven years before this day, babies in this large world of soccer. This team was extremely close. Some of us celebrated our drivers' licenses, high school graduations and college scholarships together. Others stood in one another's weddings. That closeness enabled us to pull together and fight back from adversity.

Our sense of humor was also a major asset, even though what's funny to us probably wouldn't be funny to others. We were able to joke about the tough situations, and that really helped when traveling in countries where accommodations, food and transportation were often inadequate. In that environment, stress is a major factor in your game performance. The ability to laugh at surviving on Snickers and instant oatmeal, bathing in ice water, battling diarrhea during games and enduring seemingly endless bus rides allowed us to play consistently well.

Because of our camaraderie, we believed in ourselves. We felt we could overcome anything. On the field we fought for each other. That's the difference between this team and others. We had grown up together through the years.

Little did I know after that 1991 World Cup how much growing up I had ahead of me.

Chapter 2

I Refuse to Let Them See Me Cry

After we returned from China, I threw myself into promoting women's soccer. Americans' attitudes were changing, and people wanted to talk to me and hear what makes a champion. Coming off such a high, I was surprised to learn that some of my teammates hit a depression when we returned to the States. They went back to their homes and jobs without many reminders of our great accomplishment. I didn't face that, because I immediately jumped into this new role as spokesperson for the game. It was an exciting time in my life and my soccer career. I was on cloud nine.

When I did an appearance, a presentation or signed autographs, I saw kids just light up. I saw them dreaming. I saw people thinking twice about women's soccer. The media came and asked questions when previously they didn't care. Every day, every appearance I did I felt was helpful for U.S. soccer. I was trying to be everywhere for everyone. To do everything for the sport.

But I forgot about taking care of myself.

Soon after the 1991 victory, I began to feel dizzy. I suffered from fevers, migraine headaches, nausea, sleeplessness and utter exhaustion. Some nights I would sweat through two or three T-shirts. Finally, I went to the doctor. "Take it easy," he said simply. "You've just come off a whirlwind two years: an engagement, wedding and marriage in 1990, the World Cup victory, travel, appearances. You just need a vacation."

I followed his advice and rested for two months, then jetted off to Sweden to play semi-pro there. Two miserable years later at an Olympic Sports Festival in San Antonio, I became delirious during a game. I wandered off the field in the wrong direction, and my teammates had to come and get me. It was July in Texas and 100 degrees. The trainers figured I had a muscle glycogen depletion, that there was no energy in my muscles. They stuffed me with M&Ms and Coke with packets of sugar poured in it. That didn't seem to help my symptoms, so after the game I went to the trainers' room where they suggested I eat lots and rest to replenish my starving muscles.

I tried to play two days later, and the same delirium took over. I can't remember much except that I felt disoriented, like I was drunk. After the game, I went to the training room, where I received an IV for dehydration. The next game I was still too weak to play, so I sat in the stands with my dad and watched my team collect a bronze medal. A few weeks later I was playing with the National Team in New York, and I became deranged and irrational again. I wound up in Lennox Hill Hospital for more testing. An echocardiogram and stress tests proved my ticker was fine. No one knew what was wrong with me.

Then that fall, after even more testing, I was diagnosed with mononucleosis. Finally! A name for my illness. And finally, something to fight against. But in the winter of 1993, I was diagnosed with Chronic Epstein-Barr Virus or EBV, a little-understood disease sometimes grossly misnamed "The Yuppie Flu." Then at last in the spring, the diagnosis was updated to Chronic Fatigue and Immune Dysfunction Syndrome (CFIDS). In the midst of this nightmare, my marriage also fell apart, and my husband and I filed for divorce in October of 1994.

Despite the emotional devastation of our divorce and my weakening physical strength, I tried to keep my eyes set on the 1995 World Cup in Sweden. Defending the title was our expectation. It was the world's expectation. *My focus wasn't, however, so much on winning and dominating, but on survival.* For me it was, *Can I get through this? How am I going to help my team? How am I going to play being this sick?*

I didn't let anyone know how bad I was feeling. How could I? It was almost too heavy for me to bear. I couldn't think of letting anyone else in. I was so confused about my health and what was wrong with me, I didn't have answers for myself, let alone anyone else. I had been playing this sad way for two years. *I can do two more weeks,* I told myself.

Warming up for the first game against China, I was focused on preparing my body to play. Instead of feeling ready and light though, I felt slow, off balance and as heavy as an elephant. When we finally kicked off I thought, *Thank God! I'm at the World Cup. Here we go.* I touched the ball a couple of times and then, about five minutes into the game, went back to defend a corner kick. It was a high ball into the goal box and I leapt up to head it out of there. I remember jumping up, winning it, and then the lights went out. I woke up on the ground.

I wasn't sure what was going on, but I knew I was lying in a funny position. I had to get my leg out from under me. My head was ready to explode. BOOM! BOOM! BOOM! I was trying desperately to appear normal. Apparently I answered the trainers' questions correctly, and I seemed okay to them. "Yes, I know where I am," I must have said. "You're holding up five fingers." I refused a stretcher and insisted, "I am walking off this field." I'm telling you what I was doing because other people told me. My stepmom, Sue, said that, as I hobbled off, I gave her the thumbs up, but my eyes were crossed and I was wobbling all over. I don't remember anything.

When I finally came to, I couldn't believe it. I was already struggling through so much. Now this! To be knocked out in the first minutes of the first game was agonizing. What was next for me?

A few days later, I saw a tape of the collision during an interview. It made me sick to my stomach. The camera angle was from behind the goal, so I saw the Chinese player hit me, and my head snap forward. I just dropped like a bag of flour and lay there. If I had been hit in the face, I would have been killed. It was that violent. I explained to the journalist what I thought happened and made some funny comments. Seeing what had taken place nauseated me, but I didn't show it. I felt lucky to be alive. And I was trying to be strong for my team because I knew it would bother them if they saw me upset. I didn't want to be a distraction. Plus, at that point, I *still wanted to play.*

In my journal, I wrote:

> *June 9, 1995: Had to go to the hospital for a CAT scan (Yes, I have a brain), and poor Dad was there again, scared to death for me. I swear I will put him to an early grave. He's worse than I am, on the verge of crying, trying to be brave for me. Poor Papa, I know his heart is breaking. Even Sue is crying. Anyway, head-wise I'm okay (a concussion), but the knee is painful. A sprain to the right medial collateral ligament from the way I fell. The doctor says to push through the pain for a quicker rehab. Our motto is 'Good pain is hard to find.' Appropriate. I'm running already (straight) with lots of grunting and swearing, but at least <u>running</u>. I'm trying for the quarters on Tuesday. Please God.*

I struggled at first with my new role on the bench. For a career starter, it was tough being on the sideline. When our team doctor said I was handling it like a champion, I almost cried. People thought I had it all under control, but my disappointment was very close to the surface. At any moment I felt like I'd lose it.

We defeated the Australians in the quarterfinal; the team didn't need me. I told coach Tony DiCicco that I was ready if he wanted to play me in the semi-final against Norway. Many people have criticized his decision, but I am grateful he gave me a chance. However, I would have accepted any decision, because it would have been best for the team.

While I was standing on the sideline before kick-off, Tony said he didn't expect me to fly in and rescue the team. But I thought the world did. I just wanted to make a small difference. Actually, I wanted to make a huge difference. I wanted to score goals, be a threat, be the best player out on that field. And it killed me knowing I wouldn't be that player. I hobbled around the field the best I could for 90 minutes, trying desperately to make something happen for our losing team.

The score was 1-0, and the final whistle blew. I remember thinking three things: *This can't be real. I want another chance. And I refuse to let them see me cry.* I didn't want to see myself in some soccer magazine in tears of defeat. So I just stood there, willing myself not to cry. I remember watching the Norwegians celebrate and wanting to kill them.

A few days after that, on June 18, I wrote this in my journal:

> *I'm still getting used to the idea of losing. We came out flat. Others have explained it as nervous, tentative, scared, whatever. It was not the U.S. team I know. I did my best, but on that day it just wasn't enough. My thought immediately after the final whistle was not to cry—not to show the world how much it hurt. And to get to my family.*

It was awful to shake the Norwegians' hands, to talk to the press, answering the obvious, the stupid, and the humbling questions. 'Yes, the Norwegians were better than us today. They deserved the game.' To stand there as the world watched us come up short, knowing that I will be seeing those images for the rest of my life, was excruciating.

After the warm down, I went over to the group of American fans. There were maybe 150 people standing there—all in their U.S. stuff, all dressed up with their red, white and blue. The spectacle would have been funny if it hadn't been so sad. They cheered as I came over, but I couldn't look up at them because of my tears. Everyone was crying—they all felt so badly for me. I just wanted to get to my dad and stepmom. My dad and I hugged as I sobbed and let out a choice cuss word. Right then I looked up to see my grandma standing there. Oops! "I'm sorry, Grandma," I said. She laughed and cried at the same time.

Then I walked off toward the locker room. Since I was the last player off the field, the press mobbed me and I had to be the "professional Akers" again—no tears, gracious and humble in defeat. It was hard. Even harder was the banquet honoring the world champion Norwegian team the next night. We sat in the back—unnoticed. Norway was at the head table and I had to give the Golden Boot away to this tournament's high scorer, a Norwegian. My teammate Carin Gabarra gave her Most Valuable Player award away to the new MVP, also a Norwegian, and she walked back to the table trying not to cry. Then we got out of there. I was so happy to leave. I just wanted to go home.

In the past, I'd put all my feelings of hurt, anger and disappointment in some far away closet inside me. I refused to face or even acknowledge the feelings. I wanted everyone—including myself—to believe that nothing and no one could hurt me. My experiences with CFIDS, divorce, injury and this recent loss forced me to look at things differently.

These tough and painful experiences provide the opportunity to see who you are and what you are made of. I've found that if you run or turn away, you lose. You lose because you won't face yourself. You lose because you refuse to accept the challenge of a lifetime.

Only a courageous person can accept and pursue the opportunity to face herself, to dive into a sea of hurt, unanswered questions and loneliness in order to find the light. To find answers. To find out who you are.

I don't know what you're facing today. Maybe it's a devastating disappointment like I encountered during our 1995 loss. Or it's the break up of a relationship. Maybe you're sick. Or facing the loss of someone you love. Maybe you're lonely and feeling left out. We all have those times in our lives.

Everyone has moments, days, sometimes years like this. The important thing to remember is that struggle and hardship make you stronger. The old saying is true: If it doesn't kill you, it will make you stronger. Ninety-nine point nine percent of the things we face in life will eventually strengthen us if we can hang on somehow in the meantime.

It is the hanging on that makes us tough. It is the hanging on that gives us confidence. It is the hanging on, the fight, that enables us to conquer and overcome all odds.

Something awesome will be around the corner.

Chapter 3

You Stupid Jerk

I hate to lose. That's probably no surprise. Even when I was a little girl, I hated to lose. In grade school, I raced a guy named Greg in the 40-meter dash, and when he outran me, I beat him up because I lost. Even if I lost in Monopoly, I got mad.

When I was 8 my mom signed me up for soccer. Because I was the only one unafraid of the ball and mud, the coach made me the goalkeeper. At that age, keeper was a horrid position for me because after every goal or loss—which was often—I cried. I begged my mom to let me quit. She refused. Plus our uniforms were pink and yellow. Girlie colors—the worst!

My favorite colors were the black and gold of the Pittsburgh Steelers. I sported my No. 75 "Mean" Joe Greene jersey and forest green "Toughskins" jeans with holes in the middle of the double-knee patches. My dream was to play wide receiver for the Steelers. My brother, Michael, and I would practice "hail Mary" passes in the backyard, and I imagined myself catching the winning touchdown at the Super Bowl. I also practiced with the boys at school during recess. Then one day in third grade, my gym teacher pulled me aside and said, "Girls don't play football." I was crushed. I didn't want to go with the girls' class—I wanted to play football with the boys. So I got sent to the principal's office. My mom had to come in, and while I sat in the hall, they finally agreed to let me play with the boys.

I was also as stubborn as all get out. I can remember sitting for hours at the dinner table in the dark with a plate of peas in front of me. Gosh, I hated peas. After several attempts at hiding them in my pockets, milk or mouth, I out and out refused to eat them. My parents insisted I sit at the table until my plate was clean. *Forget that*, I thought, *I'll sit here all night if I have to*. And I did—almost. Sometimes I'd see the peas still on my plate the next morning, but most times, I'd outlast my parents. Even though I missed all the good, nighttime TV shows, I wouldn't have to eat the peas.

These old stories are hilarious to look back on. Scary as it is, they still depict a lot of my current character and personality traits—both on and off the field. I still detest losing. But, I don't beat people up or cry (well, sometimes I do) if I don't win. I may *want* to crunch people, but I learned I can't do that. Now I wear the U.S.'s red, white and blue instead of pink and yellow. I still love the Steelers, but have relinquished my Super Bowl dream for the dreams of soccer World Championships and Olympic gold. And now, I like peas.

My stubbornness still gets me in trouble today, however. Due to CFIDS, it is difficult not to cross the invisible line between training and overdoing it. That is where my good friend and strength coach, Steve Slain, comes in. He has been my drill sergeant and watch dog. Together, we planned a training regimen that would not only get me fit, but also keep me healthy and at a safe pace. At first, I worked out on our program with him in the mornings. Then, I would sneak off and work out again later that day—only to get sick and disqualify me from training at all the next morning with Steve. Once he finally figured out what I was doing, I got the "you-stupid-jerk" look and the wrath of Steve!

I am also blessed with a somewhat faulty memory. OK, "airheadedness" to use the exact word of friends and family. I say blessed because even though it is embarrassing sometimes, it provides lots of laughter. When things get really bad, my friends say, "Stop by the gas station and fill your head up on air." I inherited it from my dad. He is the same way. Neither of us can remember names, dates, figures or other "important" stuff.

Once after having surgery on both knees, I went out to the store to run an errand and absentmindedly locked my keys in the car. I had to hobble home and was locked out of the house. I climbed onto the roof with my crutches and went through the upstairs bedroom window. That set off the house alarm and caused quite a stir among the neighbors. After retrieving a second key, I limped back to my car, drove home and acted like nothing had happened. I was so embarrassed I didn't tell anyone for a week!

My stubbornness—determination as I like to call it—has a good side too. It's part of being the best. You don't get to be a world champion or an Olympic gold medalist without a deep aversion to second place. This aversion to losing and determination to win have propelled me past opponents, obstacles and injury. And they have enabled me to contribute to the world's best women's soccer team—twice—and to enjoy being a world-class athlete.

I couldn't understand why a friend of mine was appalled when I told her I lost two teeth while playing for the University of Central Florida. It was a home game against North Carolina, and I went up for a header and collided with one of my teammates. I remember lying on the ground with my bleeding teammate, searching for my teeth. It was not a sacrifice to me: I could get new teeth, but I couldn't re-play that game.

That determination has also served me well in battling back from other injuries. I've had 11 knee surgeries, more stitches than I can count, ligament strains, tears and sprains, bruises and broken bones. If it's not one thing with me, it's another.

Most people think that playing on the National Team is all glamour. But in the early years, we'd return from overseas tournaments 10 pounds lighter and sick as dogs. In Taiwan, our trainer had to sew up my head with 15 stitches in our hotel room because the medical facility was inadequate. We've played on fields scattered with glass and nails. There was no money; many players had to quit their jobs to train adequately; some postponed graduate school and having children. The only people who followed us were our parents and friends. That's determination.

Once a reporter asked me why, with all the injuries I've sustained, I don't just quit. "Why would you quit something you love to do?" I answered plainly. Though my desire to win and determination are a big part of me, I have also learned that the love of the game and the challenge of excellence keep me coming back day after day. I'm not happy if I'm not racing mach five with my hair on fire. If I weren't a professional soccer player, I'd be a paramedic, firefighter or rock climber. I love to push to the edge and then teeter.

I used to believe that hard work and brute strength were my tickets to overcome anything. They had carried me pretty far up, and I counted on them like friends—hard work on one side and strength on the other. That is until I faced CFIDS. When the doctor finally told me what was wrong with me, I said, "Okay, doc, then give me a pill and let's get back to work." Even then, I believed I could work and battle my way through it.

But years later, battered by the disease, alone and depressed, I realized that no amount of force or fortitude could help me. I didn't have any anyway. I was helpless. My old friends hard work and strength weren't there for me. I had to learn a new way to cope.

One of the great life lessons I've learned through defeat and discouragement is the incredible bond it creates between people. I wrote this in my journal soon after the 1995 loss:

I've learned that making yourself vulnerable lets others in. Being strong is good, but rarely do people share with those that appear to have everything under control. I learned to loosen up, be myself. To not keep such a tight rein on my emotions, feelings and actions. I have more fun and so do those around me.

I know now that the hard times we go through are for a reason. Either to prepare you for something more difficult along down the road, to share your experience in some way to help others, or to make you take notice of your life and the changes you need to make. Without having to live with the CFIDS struggle and our divorce, I would have not been able to handle the disappointment and events at the World Cup.

███████

Chapter 4

I Never Doubted My Parents' Love

My parents were introduced by a grade-school friend of my dad's and married young. I think my mom was 19 and my dad 21. My dad was a meat cutter at a Safeway in Santa Clara, Calif., and my mom was at beauty school when they found out they were expecting me. My dad says he was scared to death, but really excited. They didn't have much money; when I was born on February 1, 1966, they had to borrow funds from my grandparents to pay the bill to get me out of the hospital.

My mom made all our clothes on her sewing machine. A big deal was going to Sears to buy "Toughskins" and "Keds" sneakers. Our house in Santa Clara was small. The homes there were built three feet apart, so you could look from your kitchen window through the next house into the third house over. Ours sat on a corner lot, so we had a big lawn, and Dad built a tree house in the backyard for us. It was the center of attraction for all the neighborhood kids.

Both my parents encouraged me and my younger brother, Michael, to do anything we wanted to do. I saw my mom, Anne, do things that average women did not do, and that made me think anything was possible. When I was in the fifth grade, she became the first woman firefighter in King County in Seattle. She has a real fire in her (no pun intended), and I definitely have that fire, too.

When I was in the fourth grade, we moved to Seattle. Dad was still a meat cutter, but he was also pursuing a master's degree in psychology in the evenings. One night I heard my parents fighting and I went downstairs crying because I was afraid they were going to get a divorce. They assured me they had no plans to split up. I believed them.

Not long after that, though, my mom and dad called Michael and me downstairs to the den. I sat on my mom's lap in the rocking chair, and she was hugging me and rocking. Then they surprised us by saying they *were* going to divorce. I was so surprised and angry they had lied. I didn't understand it.

It hit home later that rainy night when I looked out Michael's bedroom window and saw my dad carrying his pillow to his truck to leave. Then my mom came upstairs and we cried. We slept with her that night and I was very confused. My little, 10-year-old world had just been rocked. Later, I tried to hide the divorce papers in the mail from my mom. I was even angry at the attorneys.

Soon my mom started working as a fire fighter. As a fifth grader, I thought it was very cool that my mom was fighting fires while everyone else had a June Cleaver, boring mom. She had to work 24-hour shifts—24 hours on, then 48 hours off. Michael and I couldn't visit her at the fire station because she was there for work, but she would call when we came home from school. She'd put dinner in the freezer and we just helped ourselves, did our homework, played outside or whatever. She said we could sleep in her bed if we wanted to. And then Mom would be home by 8 the next morning. After the divorce, Michael and I had to learn to get by on our own. I think that's when I started to become very independent and self-sufficient.

Meanwhile, my dad was sad, and it was hard to be away from him. He made an extra effort to be at our practices, at school and visiting once a week. Through all the turmoil of the break up, I never doubted my parents' love for me and Michael. Like most kids of broken homes, we still hoped our parents would get back together. Every night I'd see my 8-year-old brother kneeling at the open window, praying for their reconciliation. I thought praying was useless. I was mad at God for hurting my brother like that. We used to go to church a lot when we lived in California, but we stopped going when we moved to Seattle. I didn't mind; I thought it was boring anyway. Church was just church and religion seemed cold, fake and hard.

At that point I did what I have done most of my life—I kept myself involved in so many different activities I didn't have to stop and deal with what was really going on inside me. By high school, I was so active with sports I didn't have time to wash my sweat socks. I lettered in soccer, basketball and softball every year, every season. And as a great athlete, I became popular. I did well in school. I liked my friends and all the activities that kept me busy, but I didn't have anyone to talk to about the turmoil going on inside or how to deal with it.

Chapter 5

The Lime-green Pick-up Truck

During my sophomore year in high school, my personal turmoil increased. I started dealing with all the typical confusion, frustration and anxiety every teenager goes through when you're trying to figure out who you are and what you want to do with your life. I explored a lot of avenues—partying, boys, skipping school, stealing. I thought those things were pretty cool, until I started getting into a lot of trouble.

I was close to getting kicked out of school and my grades were going down. My soccer suffered because I was constantly on restriction and my parents were all over my case. I was miserable and I was making everyone around me miserable too. I ignored my dad; I felt like he was trying to control me and I didn't want him (or anyone) to tell me what to do. Michael hated me because I was upsetting my dad, and he was still angry with Mom for wanting a divorce in the first place. Our house was not a fun place for me. Dad would call on the phone trying to talk to me. We'd argue and I'd yell and cry about having to miss soccer practice. Then I'd hang up on him. I was a mess inside. At times I hated stepping inside that house. I just wanted to run away.

The only person I talked to was Mr. Kovats, an English teacher and the boys' soccer coach. All the students liked him and wanted to be in his class, so I wanted to see what made him tick. Our mutual thing was soccer. To this day, I credit him with teaching me how to head the ball "cool" and to take a penalty kick. We would spend time during his free period talking about plays on the blackboard and reading soccer books. The closer we got as friends, the more I got to know what made him shine and what made him different. Mr. Kovats was a Christian, so he talked to me about his relationship with God. Besides soccer, we talked about boys, my parents' divorce, school. Everything. I was intrigued by why he was so excited about being a Christian. And why was he so happy? Mr. Kovats definitely knew something I didn't.

At times I considered becoming a Christian like Mr. Kovats, but always wound up chickening out. To me, following Christ wasn't such a great idea. As a nationally recognized athlete, I was already different. And to be different in high school was not a good thing. It was a hard thing. So to be a Christian on top of everything else scared me. I didn't want to trade my independence and personality for God's strict laws and rules. I thought the other kids would think I was a religious freak or a straight-laced geek, and I wanted to be cool.

After basketball practice one day, I finally fell apart. Mr. Kovats, who also coached the girls' basketball team, drove me home since my mom was at work. We sat in his beat-up, rusted-out, lime-green pick-up truck for the millionth time and talked. This time I cried my heart out. I hated who I was becoming, what I was doing to my family, and what was going on inside. I was angry. I was sad. I was confused. I had no one to turn to. I knew I needed something. Or someone. I told Mr. Kovats that I wanted what he had: a relationship with God.

I was still afraid of what the kids at school would think if I became a Christian, and I was afraid I wouldn't be able to be the same crazy and fun Michelle Akers. I didn't want to change my entire life. That was all true, but it wasn't the real reason I hesitated to begin a relationship with God. The real reason was this: I was just plain scared. Since my parents' divorce, I found it difficult to trust—and now to hope that what Mr. Kovats said about Jesus giving me joy was almost too much. If I committed to this and it didn't work out . . . well, that just seemed too much to risk.

But here in the rain in Mr. Kovats' lime-green pick-up truck I was at the end of my rope. I was desperate, alone and afraid. Mr. Kovats just took my hand, we bowed our heads and I repeated a prayer he said. The prayer went something like this:

"Dear Jesus, I need you. I know I cannot do it on my own. I want to know you. I want to welcome you into my life."

Immediately, I felt a rush of peace inside me. A physical feeling of warmth. I took a deep breath, and all the fear, confusion and worry left me. Mr. Kovats was one big smile. *Something* had happened, but what?

Finally, Mr. Kovats hugged me and told me he loved me. I went inside to face my angry family and the mess I had made, and to my surprise, I wasn't frustrated or scared anymore. Whoever this Jesus was would carry me through anything I had gotten into in the past. From that moment forward, I was a different person. Nothing anyone would notice at first, but in time, that moment became a turning point in who I was and how I lived my life.

The next day at school some of the Christian girls on the basketball team came up to me and excitedly said they heard I had welcomed Christ into my life. I was scared to death. How did they find out? I looked around the hall to see if anyone heard what they said. *I hope not.* I had so many fears about being a Christian and now all these people knew.

Even then I was an all-or-nothing-type person, and I was afraid I couldn't do the Christian thing completely, even though I wasn't sure what that was. The night before I had made a decision out of desperation, and the next day, I was unsure I was ready to go public with it.

Don't get me wrong. I was thrilled that I made that decision, but thought it was way too personal for them to know. I was still getting used to the idea of this Jesus and what it meant to give him your life.

I started to attend church with Mr. Kovats and his family. I really liked it. I was surprised to find that I began to understand the Bible a little bit. I met some others kids who wanted to follow Christ. Within a couple of months, my life got a whole lot better: I quit skipping school and drinking. I broke up with my older boyfriend. Because I was out of trouble, life with my family improved too. I spent time with my dad because I wanted to, not because I had to. I told him I loved him.

Things were looking up for me.

Chapter 6

I Would Have Played One-Legged

College coaches began phoning me about soccer scholarships during my senior year in high school. My club team was nationally ranked, so lots of university coaches had seen me play. I made the Olympic Development Program team, but my parents couldn't afford to send me. Fortunately, I was still recruited by UNC, University of Connecticut, George Mason and University of Massachusetts. I finally decided on the University of Central Florida. Coach Jim Rudy was excellent and I loved the successful soccer program and the people.

I remember arriving at that campus with all my stuff in the fall of 1984 and thinking, *"Oh, my gosh, I am all alone."* Seattle was a long way from Orlando, Fla. Soon I met up with goalkeeper Amy Allmann, whom I had played against for many years in Seattle, and we roomed together in the dorm.

As newcomers to collegiate soccer, we weren't used to the 5 a.m. running, training, lifting and sprints that our coach was famous for. Basically, it was a "run-until-you-drop" mentality. Although I ended up an All-American and team MVP that first year, I started the season terrified I was going to get cut. In one of our first practices, Coach Rudy rotated different defenders against me: one with particularly good speed, one who could kick you into the stands, etc. No one could stop me—not so much because I was so good, but because I was in a fearful frenzy the whole time!

It was at UCF that I started wearing number 10. Up until then, I had always worn 17. People often ask if I chose 10 to be like my idol, Pele, but the real story is that my college coach threw me jersey number 10 because it was the only one left. I've stuck with it ever since.

I was surprised not only by the conditioning in collegiate soccer, but also by the level of emotional and mental intensity. If you weren't pulling your load, the older players would get on you and tell you to get off the field. "If you aren't going to play," they'd yell in your face, "then go home!"

In my first game against our big rival North Carolina, the veterans were very nervous in the locker room. They were trying to encourage me by saying everything would be all right. I was too clueless and naive even to be nervous.

Apparently the UNC players had heard of me, because they were slamming and grabbing me all over the place. When I went up for a head ball, one Tarheel pushed me onto the Carolina-blue track and snarled, "Welcome to college soccer," as I got up. Another grabbed me from behind, threw me to the ground and broke my bra. These things surprised me, but they also got me fired up. The overt intensity and competitiveness in college soccer were new to me, but I thought it was great. I knew I had it in me too.

I also faced a new vehemence when the first National Team traveled to Italy in the summer of 1985. The other teams were much fitter and more soccer savvy than we were. Our opponents grabbed our shorts and pulled our hair on breakaways: These girls were playing for their lives and for their country. We didn't know what it was like playing for our country yet. Dressed in second-hand uniforms and purple sweats, we were more like an all-star team. No red, white and blue. Just a bunch of college girls traveling the world playing soccer.

Collegiate soccer and international experience also introduced me to one of my greatest battles: a never-ending succession of injuries. I returned from Italy to face my sophomore season with a dislocated shoulder. The trainers taped my arm to my body because any bump could pop the shoulder out again. I played a few games like that until I ripped up my knee. I also had my first of 11 knee surgeries that fall. Finally, I was red-shirted and found myself extremely frustrated to be stuck at home while my team struggled through the year.

I felt like I was always working toward the day when I could play healthy, but that day was forever dangling out of reach. I'd heal up one injury only to get whacked and injured again. Some seasons I knew the trainers at rehab better than my teammates! I played stupid sometimes too—once with a major tear to my right medial collateral ligament, so I could only play left-footed. I didn't care: I would have played one-legged if I had to. I think that kamikaze attitude is one reason I am such a well-rounded player—I had to learn to play around and despite these injuries, which helped to develop all areas of my game.

My days at UCF weren't all injuries and soccer though. Like most students far from home for the first time, I wanted the full college experience. At first, I concentrated only on school and soccer. Then I fell head over heels in love with a fourth-year football player. In high school, I went to my prom (and even wore a dress!) and I saw my friends date, but I was more interested in soccer and other activities. So this first love hit me like a Mack truck. My boyfriend introduced me to a more active social life. We did everything together.

Eventually, however, he broke up with me for another girl. I was devastated. That rejection sent me reeling. I began going out six nights a week and not getting home until 3 or 4 in the morning. I started missing class and showing up at practice still drunk from the night before. My coach knew something was wrong because I would cry at practice. I was 10 pounds overweight and my good grades slipped to D's and F's.

By the end of my junior year, I looked at myself in the mirror and wondered, *What have I been doing?* I almost lost my scholarship. And I definitely lost my self-respect. I knew I had to make some big decisions if I wanted to continue as a soccer player and respect myself as a person.

I decided to go to summer school in order to raise my grades and be eligible to play in the fall. As part of my responsibility (and guilt) for the past months of craziness, I refused to ask my parents for money and basically survived on popcorn and Kool-Aid for three months. I was glad to see that summer end! By the time fall rolled around, I had everything back on track and was ready for another great season and a more committed school year.

Soccer was my number one now and if anything was affecting my soccer, I made a change. I could handle myself now.

Chapter 7

All of a Sudden, I Was a Role Model

After I graduated from UCF in 1989, the university retired my number and I began to play for the National Team full time. I even had a stint trying out as a field goal kicker for the Dallas Cowboys. A sports agent called and invited me to a training camp in Long Beach, Calif. *What the heck*, I thought, *I don't have anything to lose.* My farthest attempt reached 52 yards. The national newspapers picked up on the story and so did *People* magazine. The possibility of becoming the first woman in the National Football League intrigued me, but I didn't want to leave behind the *real* football. My focus was not on a Super Bowl, but on the first World Cup in China. I absolutely believed that, if I set my mind to it, then I could be the best in anything I chose to do.

After college, it was difficult to find people to train with. In order to stay in shape for the upcoming championship, I had to work out alone or find pick-up games. Sometimes, I would get lucky and find some serious college guys and have a blast for a few weeks until they had to go away again. I also trained with the oldest boys at Post to Post soccer camp in the summers. The first couple days were always a "prove it" kind of competition between us—their challenging me to prove that I could play with them. Only after I beat them a few times or hung tough when they hammered me would they *just play*. It was a cool feeling each week to change kids' minds about the ability of a girl to play.

And when we won the first World Cup in China, I was excited to change the *world's* mind about women's soccer. I could never forget the feeling of scoring the winning goal for my team. Or the fireworks. Or the "U.S.A." chants of thousands of fans. Or the pride of representing my country. We had come so far since the purple sweat-suit days of 1985, getting killed by international opponents. Now we were the best in the world.

While I believed we could win it, I had no idea what that victory would do to change my life. The first inkling that something internationally spectacular had happened came the day after I returned to the States. I flew immediately to Miami for an Umbro photo-shoot at the Orange Bowl. Two of the Umbro guys were English, and they were unusually excited for me. They knew what it meant to win a World Cup.

A few days later, at the men's World Cup draw in New York City, legends of the game like Pele, Beckenbauer, and Fransie Mueller knew who I was and actually came up to *me* to give their congratulations. To have those people who set the soccer standard approach me was surprising. So was the new respect. When people stood in line to have me autograph my picture, I thought it was the weirdest thing ever.

In a matter of one month, I was placed on a pedestal and expected to be outgoing and schmooze with the soccer world. I found that difficult at times because that wasn't really my personality. I could sign autographs and smile for the camera, but standing on a stage telling thousands of people how to be great was terrifying. All of a sudden, I was a role model. I didn't ask to be a role model and I didn't know *how* to be one. I just played soccer and I was good at it. That's all. In fact, being thrust into the limelight forced me to reshuffle what I thought about soccer and where I belonged in that whole story.

I resolved to learn how to grow into this soccer persona. I tackled this new challenge like I do everything else: with my head down and barreling straight ahead. I told myself, *I'm going to work hard at this spokesperson thing.* I started really focusing on changing and promoting women's soccer around this country and the world. I did clinics, wrote articles, did interviews and made appearances. I was everywhere.

At the same time I was skyrocketing as a leader for women's soccer, my health was declining. I had returned from the 1991 World Cup exhausted. I felt like I could never get caught up on my sleep. It was almost imperceptible at first, but as time went by, I became increasingly listless and achey, like I had a never-ending battle with the flu.

I was used to being high energy, but now something inside me was changing. I slept 12 hours a night and then still needed a two-hour nap in the afternoons. For many months my strength continued to dissipate. But I kept on, and it was my "never-say-quit" mentality that slowly killed my body. That's the irony of CFIDS. The more you fight, the more it physically defeats you. I didn't know that then.

So there was a war going on between my mind and my body. My mind said, "Yes," but my body said, "No way." I would see these huge opportunities in front of me, but I couldn't get there because I was sick. I was struggling to maintain my new ambition of promoting women's soccer.

By 1993, just to make it through the day was an accomplishment. Each day I felt like I had flown to Europe, not eaten or slept, gotten right back on the plane, flown to the United States and then trained. When it was really bad, I couldn't sit up in a chair. The racking migraines stranded me at home alone, unable even to get up to brush my teeth or find something to eat. It was awful.

Unfortunately, I couldn't face the fact that my body was failing me. So I kept on keeping on. Sure, I'd had injuries before, but I always used determination and strength to fight back. Now those means didn't seem to be working. I was beginning to realize I couldn't count on my body to come through for me any more.

And that meant I couldn't count on soccer either.

Chapter 8

Will I Ever Be Me Again?

I ignored my weakening condition for a few years because I thought I could beat it. I didn't want to be a Michelle Akers who couldn't be the best in the world. I didn't want to be anyone but the stud who finished all the fitness first and could bounce back from any injury. For me to lose that persona was so scary. It was the only *me* I knew. I couldn't face giving up that identity. One day the light bulb went on and I began to understand the devestating effects of CFIDS. I wrote in my journal on March 31, 1996:

> *The last few days I have been intensely studying CFIDS and its emotional/personal effects on its victims and realized on a deeper level that this disease is not only physically debilitating and emotionally gut wrenching, but as the days and months pass by, it gradually steals away who you are—or better yet—how you define yourself.*
>
> *CFIDS cuts you to the core. It takes away all of what the world (and you) determine as successful and useful in a person, i.e., independence, work ethic, personality, energy, etc. That is why this illness is so devastating. It not only makes you sick*

*by taking away your lifestyle, career, and friends,
but it also kills your identity.*

*It cruelly grinds down everything you have been
able to rely on and trust implicitly: YOU. No longer
can you rely on your ability to perform, think, plan
or hope. For example, due to the physical effects of
CFIDS, I am limited in my duties as a soccer
player and company spokesperson. At times, my
thinking is profoundly affected; my brain is foggy
and I cannot concentrate. I am reluctant to plan
appearances or group activities ahead of time
because I don't know when I might 'crash' and,
therefore, have to beg out at the last minute. And
on the very bad days, I teeter on the edge of utter
hopelessness in my battle to overcome this dogged,
impetuous disease. Will I ever be ME again?*

On April 3, I had some more thoughts about how
CFIDS has affected me:

*I was once what you call a low-maintenance
person. No special attention or needs. Independent.
Strong. But now I need all these special
considerations, excuses, rules to live or do the
things I want to do. I am high-maintenance.
Fragile. For example, to play for the National
Team is tough. Sometimes I can practice and
sometimes not. Not very reliable. I hate getting
sympathy for feeling awful, yet I want people to
understand how bad I feel and that I'm not just
copping out. I want to train, I just don't have the
gas to get the job done and still be able to function
at the end of the day. I dread having to tell the
coaches I can't practice . . . and the thing is I can
practice, but if I do, I'll feel awful and then,
tomorrow I'll feel even worse. So, technically, I can,
but I won't. I hate that.*

*I'm starting to realize that just as I've had to
adapt my 'person' to this disease, so will I have to
adapt Michelle the Soccer Player to CFIDS. I can*

no longer be the fittest, strongest, quickest all the time. I have to choose my moments. Pray for those moments to be there when I need them. If CFIDS is running its course that day or week, I can't think right. I am slowed and fatigued. I have nothing to offer my team, except maybe my presence. Is that enough?

In the meantime, I can change the kind of player I am when I am healthy and conserve the explosiveness and energy for the days and games to come. Be smart. Be savvy. Skillful. Let the ball do the work as they say. Be a veteran and orchestrate the game. Take it over mentally. Can I do that?

Two days later:

Well, things have certainly gotten better health-wise. I took a couple of days off and, Voila! I feel better. It's just getting through those tough couple of days that's the tricky part.

It took me years to realize that CFIDS isn't something you get over. I may never get physically better from this thing. You have it, to one degree or another, for the rest of your life. It also took me years to realize I wasn't going to be able to kick this by myself. In May of 1996, for International CFIDS Awareness Day, I wrote a statement for Congress (see Appendix B). That statement was basically my acceptance of this illness for life. It was my acceptance of God's plan for my life: that I could be special and *not* be the stud soccer player I was used to being.

But for five excruciating years before I came to those conclusions, my life was agonizing. CFIDS had taken everything away from me: my career, my health, my sense of self. It took my energy. I was sick 24 hours a day. I could not have one moment of respite from feeling terrible. I felt like I was carrying a truck on my back all day.

I decided I couldn't go on like that. I was emotionally at the end. I was spiraling into greater and greater despair. I was lost. If I was going to get better, I had to make some big decisions.

Chapter 9

Never in a Million Years

While my health was declining, my 1990 marriage was running a parallel route downward. I finally hit rock bottom completely when we filed for divorce in mid 1994. My dream was to get married and live happily ever after. Isn't that the way it's supposed to happen? When the promise of that dream was broken, I was crushed.

My journal from that time shows a lot of confusion and sadness:

August 26, 1994:

> *It's late or early, depending on the person: 1 a.m. I can't sleep again. Almost every night I wake up or can't get to sleep. This decision is taking its toll. I can't stop my mind from racing about the details of moving out, divorce, examining my feelings. It's driving me nuts.*

> *The act of breaking up this part of my life is painful and exhausting. I think I will rest easier once everyone knows. I* _hope_ *so anyway. I don't know how I'll tell my grandma and grandpa. They're about to celebrate their 50th wedding anniversary. I can't wait to talk to Dad more about*

it. He always helps me, no matter how clouded my thinking may be.

I feel weird thinking of myself as divorced. I think about the moment when I will take off my wedding ring, what I will do with my engagement ring, and how I will break it to the team. A lot to be strong for.

My range of feelings is incredible. I am afraid. I am excited to have a new future. I am sad. I am ready to move on. I feel lost and alone. I cry a lot. I feel the love and support of my family and friends.

I never imagined in a million years I would be getting a divorce. Live and learn. And never say never.

Nothing could help me out of this pit: not my career, not my health, not my relationships. Nothing. It finally got to the point where everything was gone and I couldn't go to a part of my life that was right. In the past, if I had an injury and couldn't play, I'd focus on partying. If I was healthy, soccer was my number one. Now I had nothing.

I'd struck up a friendship with a strength coach named Steve Slain in Orlando. He reminded me of Mr. Kovats: kind, gentle and with that same inexplicable draw. He, too, was excited about his relationship with God. Steve studied the Bible on his own in the mornings and was fired up about going to church. Sometimes I'd go with him. I had forgotten about being a Christian, but I think deep down I knew my focus had been wrong for a great many years. I didn't always want to go to church, but I knew I *needed* to be there.

I then decided to go to my family's cabin in Seattle. The move toward divorce had been so difficult that I needed to sort things out. I wanted to be near my family and knew I needed to be still just to figure out what was going on. With my life, my health, my future. I decided I couldn't afford *not* to feel. I needed to be sad—to experience my feelings and work through them. *If I don't handle this differently*, I thought, *I will never be able to recover.*

Even though I couldn't put it into words at the time, I had this big feeling inside that I needed to get things right with God. I hadn't spent much time thinking about spiritual things since I was in high school and Mr. Kovats introduced me to his faith in Christ. I still went to church on Easter and Christmas, but I didn't bring religion into my daily life. God was definitely not a part of my marriage nor my soccer career. I threw up a prayer here and there for help or strength or a team win. But I made my own decisions and dealt with the consequences; and I thought I had done a pretty good job of keeping things under control. Until now.

There in the cabin I was still so sick; I couldn't take a five-minute walk without needing two days on the couch to recover. I was forced to spend a lot of time thinking about who I was. That was the hardest thing. It scared me to death. This time I couldn't distract myself with soccer, running, lifting or partying because I was so ill. I was forced to lie there and look at my life. I didn't like what I saw.

At that point, I was glad to give God anything he wanted. "You can have this stuff," I said. "You can have this body. You can have this life. You can have *me*. Because I've made a mess of everything."

I called Mr. Kovats to ask him how I could start learning about God and how to be close to him again. He suggested reading the Bible and praying. I tried doing what he said, but it all meant nothing to me. I felt nothing inside. No love. No peace. No change. I was frustrated and hopeless. *This God thing is not working*, I thought.

Then Steve sent me some tapes from his church in Orlando. The messages were about relationships with other people and with God. The preacher talked a lot about love. I know it sounds odd, but I think those tapes are what began to redirect me. The music and singing brought me peace. I remember sitting by a big river feeling joyful. Prior to hearing those tapes, I was all jumbled up inside, confused, frustrated and disjointed. Now I had a ray of hope.

Soon after, I went to church with my grandparents in Seattle, and we heard the preacher talk about God's call on people's lives. I had a strong sense in my mind that that was what God wanted *me* to do too: tell others about him.

I said, "Uh uh! No way!" At first, I tried to ignore this sense, but it kept coming back stronger and more vividly each time. I was having an internal battle with God: "I could never in a million years do that. I don't want to do anything special for you. I want to sit here in this pew and be like everyone else."

I was so freaked out that I fled the church and called Steve from a pay phone on the way home. I told him what I thought God wanted me to do. I was freaking out. Me? Talk about God to other people?

I was scared to death at the thought of being a "spiritual nut." That was one of my fears: what would my friends, fans and the world think of me? Me—the tough, independent, strong soccer player—reading the Bible and preaching the gospel. Never in my wildest dreams did I think of myself as a leader for Christ. My other worry was this: How could I still be Michelle Akers, enjoy life, be a fun person, and also follow God? So many rules and so many high expectations. I was afraid I'd have to put on the nun outfit to be a true Christian.

Steve calmed me down, but I was still worried about what God had shown me. How could I be a leader for him? Me? A leader for God? Ha!

Chapter 10

Here I Am

I returned to Orlando from the Seattle cabin with a renewed spirit. My emotions were still like a roller coaster and my health continued to falter, but my heart felt new. I started to put the pieces of my life back together. I got my own apartment and began going to church regularly. It took months of hard work, agonizing prayer and lots of crying, but that peace I had known in high school began to return. I knew it had to do with inviting God back into my life, but I wasn't always sure what to do to cultivate that relationship. I was just glad to have peace and to know that I was on the right track again.

As you know by now, I am a very stubborn and independent person—which has been a great strength, but it is also weakness. It's a weakness because I think *I* have all the answers. I can do it. I don't need help from anyone. Looking back, I think God was gently, patiently tapping me on the shoulder and calling my name for years. But I continuously brushed him off, saying, "Hey, I know what I am doing. I can make these decisions. Leave me alone." Then I think he finally said, "OK," crossed his arms and looked at me sadly—because he knew where I was going and that I was going to make a lot of mistakes by ignoring him. He knew I would be hurting in the future.

It took total devastation before I would acquiesce and say, "OK, God. You can have my life." It took everything crashing down—it took my becoming nothing; flat on my back unable to make decisions coherently; unable to go for a walk; unable to distract myself in any way—before I came crawling back to God, pleading, "Please, help me."

But it wasn't a punishment. I am not bitter about any of this stuff. It was a wake-up call. Some people take a tap on the shoulder; I needed a sledgehammer to the head! God was saying to me, "Pay attention! This is important! You can't do it on your own. Rely on me and I will give you what you need."

God's been lifting me out of my mess day by day ever since I made the decision to welcome him back in my life. He loved me when I couldn't even love myself. It hasn't been a sudden, magical rescue. It has been day by day—gradually changing my focus, learning about who God is, surrounding myself with other Christians, finding a church that would teach, uplift and guide me.

All those fears about rules and giving up Michelle Akers have subsided or *are subsiding.* I've even lost interest in maintaining parts of the old me. I can't wait for him to change those parts of me that always get me in trouble: my pride, stubbornness and independent will to do things *my* way. I have changed a lot, and a big change is in the things that are missing: fear, loneliness and frustration.

I've discovered that there are indeed rules to obey, but I *want* to do it. I used to cringe when I heard the word "obey," but I'm learning that God does not want me to be respectful of his ways in order to squash me or put me in a box. He wants me to be happy. God's guidelines are to protect and provide for me. Since he created me, he knows what's best for me. I obey out of my love and trust of Christ. I know I can't do it by myself and I don't want to. I don't have all the answers, so I defer to someone who has the perfect answer every time.

I've found that life is more exciting God's way. It's even more of a challenge, because my dreams are so small compared to his. But the thing that makes God really cool is that, even though there have been moments when I thought it couldn't get worse, I eventually found out that I could rest, be at peace and be happy—*despite my circumstances.* I could actually have joy in my heart and not have things going my way.

That is definitely the story of what happened at the 1995 World Cup, when I was knocked unconscious in the first few minutes. When I joined reality the next day or so, I realized the tourney was probably over for me. Four years of daily training. CFIDS. A divorce. And now this. What else was going to come my way? It was a terrible blow.

Twelve family members and friends had traveled all the way to Sweden to see me play. My dad watched me in disbelief and agony. After all these adverse circumstances, here was his little girl beat up and out of the biggest tournament in the world. He cried more than I did. I tried to tell him I was OK with it, but under the circumstances, there was no way he believed me. Too much had happened and I had lost too much.

Amazingly enough, I was truly at peace. Yes, it was hard. Yes, I was disappointed. But I knew this circumstance was for a reason. What reason? I didn't know at the time. I simply understood this was out of my control and I gave it to God.

When I returned to Florida, though, I cried about it almost daily. I was sad that we lost, sad for not being able to compete and sad about the criticism we received from our country. So again I brought it to God: "I accept this situation, but how do you want me to use it? What is it all for?"

Pretty soon I got an answer. It finally dawned on me that all this tough stuff—CFIDS, divorce, World Cup injury—strengthened my dependence on and faith in

Christ. All these things gave me a story to tell about the most important thing in my life. Not soccer. Not relationships. Not my health. Yes, these are important, but not *the* most important. Christ is the most important. I've finally learned that he is the only one who is never going to let me down. Everything else has failed me.

I don't know where my life will take me, but I do know that I am equipped (or will be equipped) to do what God wants me to do. I know I will fail at times; and it doesn't mean I will be pain free and 100 percent happy all the time. But it does mean that I am not alone. It does mean that I have the strength and courage to come through any circumstance. In fact, one of my favorite Bible verses says: "Be strong and courageous. Do not be terrified; do not be discouraged, for the Lord your God will be with you wherever you go." Powerful.

That's why I am here today. Look at me: When I first realized God wanted me to be a leader for him, I panicked and pleaded to be just another face in the crowd. "No way I can do it," I said. "Pick someone else! I don't have the words. I don't know the Bible. People will make fun of me." I had a million excuses and fears.

But after awhile, I began to learn and grow. And I began to see what was possible through him and the talents he had given me. And here I am.

I tell you all this to encourage you to consider Christ. He is the only answer. I know what it's like to be sitting there and reading this stuff. It's hard to believe. But if you want *truth*: This is it!

I can truly and honestly say this because I have been at the top and I have been at the bottom. I am a world champion and a gold medalist, but in the whole scheme of things, those accolades are not important. The most important thing is giving your life to Christ and following him. That is the only way anyone is going to be happy. That is the only way you or anyone is going to find peace and joy.

A college student once told me that he wanted to give himself to God, but he didn't know how. This is what I told him:

"You give yourself to God by first realizing you can't live life fully without him. That you need him. That you believe he sent his son, Jesus Christ, to die for you, so you can receive his gift of life—joy, strength, peace, love—of salvation and a place in heaven. You just tell him what's in your heart and he will be there for you. Always.

"Once you have given yourself to him, know that all your problems do not end immediately. It is up to us to pursue God, to get to know him. You do that by spending time with him (praying), reading the Bible, learning through study books, going to church, being with other Christians. Slowly, you will discover the incredible things he has for you. He will respond, but in his time. It takes patience, and it takes determination.

"My life changes when I do as he says. When I spend time with him, something inside changes, and I am becoming someone else. Someone more like Christ. You'll soon notice that the 'practical fulfillment' of your decision to follow and believe in Christ just happens. You—and others—will see it in your daily life. It's like I can go through anything and feel this peace, power and strength inside. It's him."

(There's a more detailed explanation of how to meet Christ in Appendix C.)

My preacher, Dr. Joel Hunter, has had a profound effect on my thoughts about Christ and my relationship with God. I know it sounds crazy, but in some Sunday services, out of all the hundreds of people in there, Joel looks *right* at me. He leans over and looks right into my eyes. It makes me smile sometimes and other times, it makes me squirm. I think, *Oh no! Why is he looking at me? Now what!?*

What he said one Sunday pierced my heart. While leaning so far toward me I thought he'd fall into the audience, Joel read the questions and doubts in my heart.

He said: "Forget about what others think. Forget about the logistics of how or why. Put your eyes on God. Listen and learn. Trust. Just go out and do it."

So here I am.

Chapter 11

Now is the Time

The highlight of my re-found spiritual life and continued physical struggles culminated at the 1996 Olympic Games. Three months prior to the first-ever women's soccer Olympic venue, I was told to consider retiring because the result (including permanent damages) of playing at this level with CFIDS was unknown. It might be too much to risk. For the first time, I seriously considered, and surprisingly accepted, the fact that I would have to give up the game I loved after the Olympics.

While the National Team and I were at training camp in San Diego, I was reading up on CFIDS. A lot of the information from the controversial book *Osler's Web* was scaring the bejeebers out of me. It seemed to be all bad news and despair, and I was still struggling terribly to continue to play and train.

However, despite the book's bad news, it did give me a dim ray of hope—a doctor named Paul Cheney who had a passion for his work and possibly a few suggestions. I called him, and he recommended I try a 10-week "elimination diet." That meant eliminating dairy, caffeine, red meat, gluten, sugar. In other words, anything that was fun and good to eat. No more TCBY,

Cinnabons, pizza or my beloved Starbuck's coffee. Eager to get started, I threw out everything in my cupboards, fridge and freezer and began the diet in earnest. I did cheat on one thing: my morning cup of java!

My diet was reduced to potatoes, veggies, rice, chicken, seafood, handfuls of supplements and juice from two pounds of carrots a day. Two weeks into the diet, I started noticing some changes. I had more energy, but I was too afraid to attribute the differences to the diet. Soon I was feeling as healthy as I'd been since 1991.

Within a week of contacting Dr. Cheney, I received a phone call from a specialist at Johns Hopkins named Peter Rowe, who would "bet his house" that I had a blood pressure disorder called Neurally Mediated Hypotension (NMH), which is common in CFIDS sufferers. He offered me a test as quickly as I could get to Baltimore. I was later diagnosed as symptomatic to NMH, and we began to search for treatments that would help relieve some of my debilitating symptoms. I couldn't believe it! Dr. Cheney and now, Dr. Rowe.

And I couldn't believe God's timing. All of a sudden, I could play. It seemed I had my career back, and I was starting to have fun again on the field. Before the first two weeks of the diet, I was barely surviving each practice, and some days I got to our training center just to turn around with a massive migraine. Each day, I wondered which Michelle Akers would show up to play. But then the amazing changes began. So, with only eight weeks of real training, I was on my way to the Olympics. The last day of the 10-week diet fell on July 21—which was our opening Olympic match!

The team traveled by chartered bus from our training center in Sanford, Fla., to the Olympic village at my alma mater, UCF, escorted by nine motorcycle cops and police with sirens and lights. Traffic parted like the Red Sea and, all of a sudden, we were somebody special—Olympic athletes! I'd finally made it.

Everywhere we stayed, drove or played, the security was outrageous. Awesome, in fact. We had FBI, state patrol, riot police, state marshals, SWAT teams, and canine units. You name it, we had it. To and from our games we were escorted by police. At practices, we had SWAT teams surrounding the field and helicopters flying overhead. Guards marked the entrances and exits. The men and women on these units were incredible; we never had a worry or doubt about out safety. They became some of our biggest fans!

The team flew up to Atlanta for the Opening Ceremonies, but I decided to stay behind. Our first game was just two days away, and I feared the travel and late night could zap my needed energy for the tourney. I tried to stay up and watch my friends jaunt down the ramp in the red, white and blue garb, but I fell asleep by 10 p.m.

Our first game was at the Orlando Citrus Bowl. My family and friends were in the audience. My home town of 11 years. My home crowd. My own health seeming to return. What could be better?

After the pre-game rituals of warm-ups, meetings, bathroom breaks, taping and stretching, we walked out for the anthem. In the locker room everyone has her own routine in order to prepare herself, but eventually, we all end up in the same place—the tunnel, waiting for game time. This was a special time for me. We stood together high fiving, giving encouragement and, in general, whooping and hollering about how awesome we were and what we were about to do to our opponent. The feeling between us was one of intensity and extreme confidence. We stood as a team totally calm, fired up. Ready. I absolutely believed we were going to win it all.

When we walked out in our white jerseys to the Olympic theme, I was barely holding it together emotionally. Talk about goose bumps! That moment was awesome. I looked for Dad in the audience and gave him the usual thumbs up. Then when the whistle blew, nothing else existed except the field and what was happening during that game. It was back to business. Play the game, win, and focus on the next opponent.

We beat Denmark in 102-degree heat, 3-0. I felt and played well. When coach Tony DiCicco pulled me in the 76th minute to rest for the remaining tourney, my hometown crowd gave me a standing ovation. It was absolutely incredible, so satisfying and overwhelming to see the many people who had supported me over the years, helped put me back together, and cheered for me. Now they were able to see firsthand the impact of their time and energy: an Olympic athlete. And maybe a gold medalist.

In the next two matches, we beat Sweden and tied China in order to move to the semi-final against our old nemesis, the Norwegians. The crowds at all these matches were absolutely tremendous in both numbers and sheer enthusiasm. Many fans have asked about the "Moomba" sign we carried to each venue. The term means "to celebrate." We picked it up at a team building exercise before the Games began. One fan carried the sign all the way to Athens, Ga., for the final games. It became a tradition for us to find the sign before each match.

While I felt better than I had in years, the demand of the games and the stifling heat took its toll. After each game, I had to have IVs—a needle to put two or three liters of saline back in my body, because I couldn't hydrate myself properly. Another needle drained my knee. I was banged up; they had to tape me up in so many places, our trainers joked that I was usurping half the U.S. Soccer Federation budget on tape alone. Although I had been concerned about the preparation demands of my elimination diet, I didn't need to be worried. We had the best chefs and I was spoiled rotten. Gluten-free banana pancakes became the favorite of the tournament!

Since we had lost to Norway the previous year at the World Cup in Sweden, we had some special feelings about them. We walked out to a crowd of almost 75,000 people, ready to play an opponent who had been better than us one year before. We had a statement to make.

The Norwegians scored first and it seemed the World Cup champs would again defeat us. But with just 15 minutes remaining, we found our chance to tie. A blatant foul within the goal box gave us a penalty kick. No one was stepping up to take the shot, so I said, "This baby is mine." I placed the ball at the mark and squared off against their goalkeeper. Later, people asked if I was aware of the importance of that moment. I *knew* that, if I missed this shot, then we'd lose that game and be out of the Olympics. I *knew* that this would forever be a defining moment in my career and our team's history.

Incredibly, I was totally calm. I *knew* I would make it. I decided to slam it to the left corner, thinking that if by chance she got a hand on it, she would go in the net with the ball. I blasted it just as I planned, and the goalkeeper dived harmlessly the other way.

At the end of regulation time, the score remained 1-1. I staggered off the field completely exhausted. I told Steve, our strength coach, that I couldn't make it to overtime; I had nothing left.

"Yes, you *will* make it," he countered. "Your team needs you." Steve began furiously rubbing and stretching my legs to promote energy. Lying on my back, I gulped Powerade and chomped PowerBars while my teammates joined hands and huddled above my head, strategizing and giving our team cheer.

Thankfully, just minutes into overtime, Shannon MacMillan put away the game winner. I was near collapse. With Steve's help, I left the field. After a few liters of intravenous saline and a good night's sleep, I felt better. I just thanked God for the opportunity to be there, to contribute to my team, and to face the Chinese in the final. One more to go!

Four days later, we met the Chinese in the first-ever women's Olympic soccer final. The crowd numbered 76, 481—the most ever to watch a women's competition of any kind in the world. Some of the spectators paid more than $100 for their tickets. The Chinese came out strong, but so did we. However, 10 minutes into the game, I was dragging. Somehow I managed to last until the half, the scored tied at 1-1.

We bounced back as Tiffeny Milbrett scored in the 68th minute to hold on for the prize. In the last few minutes, it was agonizing to look at the ref and watch the scoreboard clock tick down: waiting, waiting, waiting. Finally, the game was over. I raised my arms in the air, looked to the heavens, and screamed in victory and relief. It was over! We had done it! I could finally rest. God had given me a truly miraculous experience and a very special gift.

We had to go in the locker room and put on our special ceremony sweats. Then we marched out and they announced us as the Olympic gold medalists. The podium is a moment many dream about. It is *exactly* as you imagine it. Almost surreal. Extremely emotional. Tears. Laughter. Disbelief. Joy. All at once and all overwhelming. My first thought when they placed that gold medal around my neck was, *Wow! That's heavy*, then, *Wow! That's shiny*, and finally, *Wow! This is MINE*.

Standing there on the podium was a moment I had dreamed of for years. And now it was real. I stood there trying to soak up every feeling, image and thought, wanting to immortalize and memorize this once-in-a-lifetime moment. *Christ must really be in me*, I thought. Because a year ago—injured at the World Cup with a concussion—I was sick and distraught, but I felt a surprising peace. And now I'm standing on this podium with a gold medal around my neck, and I feel the same peace inside.

Then they played our national anthem. Whoa. I had watched so many other athletes sing their anthems and often wondered how I would react. What would I do if I won? I put my hand on my chest, found the American flag atop the stadium, struggled not to cry, and belted it out!

After the ceremony, I returned to the training room to load up on IV fluid while my teammates went to the post-game party. I didn't arrive at the event until 3 a.m. and was too sick to celebrate, but it didn't matter. I had what I wanted, and the people I love most were with me.

It was incredible to win the gold medal. It is a special achievement and experience. Like all the other tournaments I've played in, win or lose, I take away something more than a trophy or title. I discovered the memories and experiences of the Olympics are less about winning and more about people. I learned that all of us—fans, family, friends, chefs, volunteers, police, officials, sponsors—are part of the team. It took all of these people to win.

The Olympic Games are also about conquering obstacles. It's about incredible passion, fire, desire. It is about becoming more than you are. By reaching for our dreams, we inspire others to reach for theirs.

The day after our gold-medal win, I wrote this in my journal:

> *August 2, 1996. My thoughts are scattered and disjointed, but the sentiment and unforgettable memories will forever be embedded in my heart. My mind keeps returning to the past few years when I thought I was so alone, so isolated in my struggles and pain. God is so good. Through it all, he was preparing me for this moment, this experience. So faithful. He took it all away, but he gave me back so much more.*
>
> *I go to bed tonight an Olympic Champion.*

Appendix A

Photo Gallery

The following photographs help tell Michelle's story. From the champion's first soccer team outfitted in pink and yellow to her Olympic gold-medal game, each shot brings you face to face with Michelle Akers.

Above: My first team, the Police Athletic League Cougars. I am in the front row with the long braids. My mom, who was also my first coach, is in the back with the bandana on her head. She learned about soccer from reading library books.

Left: The Shorelake Thunderbirds was one of my club teams in Seattle. We won numerous state and regional championships together

Photo by Joanie Komura

Right: I played at Shorecrest High School from 1980-1984. In 1984 (when this photo was taken), I had a badly sprained ankle and I was questionable to play. Thankfully, our trainer taped me from ankle to knee, and I was able to play each match of the state championship. We won the state title that year.

Below: After college, I played for Tyreso FF in Stockholm, Sweden. I went there for the competitive leagues and excellent coaching. My participation in this league led to my growth as one of the best players in the world.

Photo by Bjorn Tilly

— 61 —

Right: I first met Pele when I signed with Umbro USA in the summer of 1991. I was the first woman to have a soccer endorsement in this country. In this shot, I may look calm, but I am totally freaking out because my idol gave me one of his original New York Cosmos jerseys signed, "To Michelle with love, Pele."

Left: Our 1991 team is celebrating my winning goal at the World Cup. The goal was made with just two minutes left in the final game against Norway and made for a dramatic, story book finish.

Photo by Phil Stephens

Photo by Phil Stephens

Here it is! The first ever Women's World Championship trophy. A moment I will never forget.

Photo by Joanie Komura

Above: Here I am in 1992 at one of my speaking engagements. At first, I hated and feared getting up in front of people, but over the years I have grown to love it. I look at it as the chance to change people's minds and attitudes, inspire kids to dream and achieve, and educate the world about the game of soccer and my Christian faith.

Right: The ref blew the whistle and we were out of the 1995 World Cup. In this photo, I am standing in disbelief and willing myself not to cry.

Photo by Phil Stephens

Above: What awesome dudes! Doc Mark Adams (on the left) was our team doctor for the Olympics and Steve Slain is our strength coach and massage therapist (he also works for the Orlando Magic). They were responsible for putting me back together day after day.

Above: (From left to right) My aunt Gini, Grandpa (nice hat), Grandma and Mom with their sign at the Olympics. It helped me find them in the midst of more than 76,000 fans at the final.

"Olympic Champions"

Photo by Phil Stephens

Above: My brother, Mike, me, Dad, and Sue-Sue (my step-mom) at the gold medal, post-game party. What a trip. My dad and Sue likened the tournament to reaching for the summit of a mountain—step by step. Here we are at the summit.

Below: This is the infamous Bob Costas interview where I blurted out, "Do you see this?! It's the Gold Medal, baby!!" I was delirious with joy.

Photo by: Mike Stahlschmidt ©Sideline Sports Photography

On the podium, at last. We celebrate as a team our new title as Olympic gold medalists. A historic moment for American and women's soccer . . . and an unforgettable moment in my life and career.

Photo by: Phil Stephens

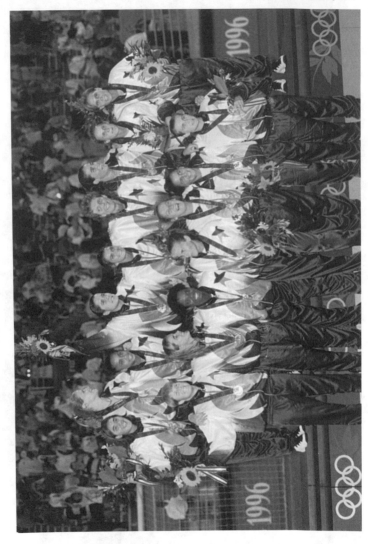

This is the dude! Mr. Kovats. He is the one who inspired me to trust, love, and walk with Someone who has forever changed my life. You go, Ko!

Appendix B

CFIDS Testimony Before Congress

In 1991, I was named the best women's soccer player on this planet, and my team, the United States of America, became the first ever FIFA women's World Champions. We went undefeated in the tournament and I scored an unprecedented 10 goals in five games.

It wasn't long after the World Cup that I began to notice a change in my energy. Over a two-year period, almost imperceptibly at first, I began to fade. Finally, I collapsed and became delirious on the field during the 1993 Olympic Sports Festival. The doctors thought at first that it might be muscle glycogen depletion, then a heart dysfunction, and finally, after collapsing yet again, I was tested for the Epstein-Barr Virus. My numbers were sky high. Bingo. We had found the culprit. Or so I thought. I was diagnosed with Chronic Epstein-Barr Virus which was later revised to Chronic Fatigue and Immune Dysfunction Syndrome (CFIDS). In 1994, three years later, I finally had a name to the thing I had to fight to regain my health.

My name is Michelle Akers. I am 5'10" and weigh 150 pounds. I am muscular. I am tan. I have wild, sun-bleached curly hair. My teammates call me "Mufasa" from "The Lion King." I love to laugh. On vacations, I love to hike the Cascade Mountains near Seattle with my dad and brother. I am the starting center forward for the world-class American women's soccer team . . . and soon to be a 1996 Olympian.

If you saw me today, you would see a healthy, physically fit, elite athlete. But I'm not. I am sick. And I am hanging on by the very will and courage that helped me attain my status as an elite athlete. Some days it is all I can do to get through the day, let alone be an elite athlete. On those days, the only way to step on the field is to stop, close my eyes, take a deep breath, and gather every ounce of strength and will, focusing solely on surviving the hour and a half of practice ahead of me. Most days, I survive the practice—sometimes, I do even better than survive and actually see glimpses of the player I used to be. Those days are glorious. To feel good. To have energy. To be light and strong. This is what it's supposed to be like. Fun. And carefree. I revel in the feeling and the gift of good health.

On the very bad days, it is all I can do to survive. I walk off—drag myself off the field, my legs and body like lead. God, they seem to weigh so much. My breathing is labored. It is all I can do to get to the locker room, change my clothes, and keep from crying from utter exhaustion and weariness. I am light-headed and shaky. My vision is blurred. My teammates ask me if I am OK, and I nod yes. But my eyes tell the truth. They are hollow, empty. Dull and lifeless. It scares me to look in the mirror when I get like this. I shake my head, knowing I overdid it again. I crossed that invisible line between functioning and being very, very sick. How long will it take to recover from is one?

I slowly get to my truck and concentrate on the road, willing myself to keep moving, not to pull over and rest. Almost there, I tell myself, *Just a few more minutes.* By the time I arrive home, I leave my bags in a pile by the door and collapse on the couch. I have no energy to eat. To shower. To call someone for help.

I tell you these things not to gain sympathy, but so you too can experience a day in the illness. Experience the pounding migraine headaches that can incapacitate me for days. The insomnia that plagues me even though I am exhausted. The overwhelming fatigue that keeps me from going to a movie or dinner with friends because I don't have the energy to talk, sit up or eat. The GI upset has caused me to go on an extreme gluten-free, dairy-free, caffeine-free, sugar-free and alcohol-free diet in hopes of finding relief or possibly a cure for the fogginess that causes me to lose concentration, and forget where I am or how to get someplace that I've been a thousand time before.

This illness demands attention in every detail of my life and if I don't pay attention, it punishes me. Without remorse. It is a difficult experience to explain because it encompasses so much of my being—of who I am. There is grief in realizing you will never be the person you were before the illness. CFIDS becomes who you are at times. Leaving you—the old you—a mere shadow.

I have always believed that you can accomplish anything through hard work and perseverance. Through dedication and commitment. This is how I became a world champion and an Olympic athlete. That is the irony of the illness. The harder you work, the more it drags you down. The more it disables you. It is the first time in my life I have been beaten. It is the first time in my life I may have to quit before I accomplish my goal. I cannot defeat this illness through hard work, or pure drive and desire. It is the first time I cannot overcome on my own terms, in my own strength.

And I am a fortunate CFIDS sufferer. Because I am an elite athlete, I have access to the best doctors, the best care in the United States and, therefore, the world. I have an incredible support system through my team and family. For example, my team is going to join me in my new gluten-free diet one evening. They help me with my bags when traveling. They force me off the field when I am pushing too hard. They drive me home when I can't make it myself. My friends pray for me daily and lift me up when I am at the end of myself.

My family, friends, coaches and employers (U.S. Soccer Federation and Reebok) are sympathetic and flexible in regards to my health and limitations. They have never doubted that I am sick, and not just depressed, mentally unstable, or God forbid, faking it.

Yes, I have lost a lot. Yes, CFIDS is a devastating disease. And no, I am not the same person before I was stricken with CFIDS and probably will never be. But this is not a message of hopelessness or defeat. It is a story about courage, growth and challenge. This is a story about overcoming. I have gained a lot from this illness. Nothing that can be touched or measured, but through the suffering and heartache, I have gained a strength and purpose that carries me when I cannot do it myself. I have seen and experienced God's grace and peace only because I have been in the valley. I now know it took this long visit in the depths of this illness to open myself to a more meaningful and purposeful life.

I live by the verse in 2 Corinthians which says, "My grace is sufficient for you, for my power is made perfect in weakness . . . . that is why, for Christ's sake, I delight in hardship . . . in difficulties. For when I am weak, then I am strong." Through God, through this weakness—this illness—God's power rests in me, and I am strong. His power is made perfect in me. I will overcome but not through any effort of my own. That is the final irony. The more I struggle to save myself from this disease, the more it takes my life away. The moment I just rest in the strength of God's perfect grace is the moment I begin to overcome.

I have learned to accept CFIDS as an opportunity to make a difference. I have turned this weakness into a strength. And even though it is still raging inside me, I refuse to be beaten by it.

I will overcome. And I will show others how to overcome also. Thank you. *(May, 1996)*

Appendix C

Face to Face with God

Hey there!

I am so glad you turned to this page! It has been our hope that my story would not only encourage, enlighten, and inspire you to persevere despite long odds or tough times, but also intrigue you enough to take one step closer to knowing God.

The most wonderful thing I have learned since I gave my life to Christ is that this Christian stuff not only creates and inspires a power within and a passion for life, but this Christian stuff is also personal, alive and real. I was just about knocked off my rocker when I first realized something so completely opposite to my past impressions of God and his followers. You see, I thought of God in relation to the churches I had attended as a kid: hard, wooden benches, stiff and boring preachers, and judgmental, prim and proper, lifeless followers. Certainly not a God or a group of people that I could relate to, live up to, or even want to be around. No joy, no hope, no fun! If that was the kind of God they followed and that was how Christians were supposed to act, I thought, then I could do much better on my own.

Unfortunately, I still come across those stiff and joyless church-goers of my childhood. But, the sad thing for them and the good news for us is they have totally missed the point! Being a Christian is not about rules, or acting a certain way, reciting Bible verses, or knowing all the hymns at Sunday service. Being a Christian is about knowing a living and breathing God. Being a Christian means throwing your head back, charging through, over, and around the impossibilities of life and living each day to its fullest in the knowledge and confidence that God is with you.

This truth is important for me to convey because it is something I missed for many years. I think it took me so long to get because, in short, I thought I knew everything. I thought I had all the answers, the strength, the way to do things, and the means to know joy, happiness and success in life. But, boy was I wrong! When all resources failed, and I stood alone looking for something to bail me out, I was forced to acknowledge the fact that there is something more to this life than me and my now-inadequate resources.

When I really started to look at the scheme of life closely, I thought: *I can't just be here to win soccer trophies and championships.* I mean, when it's all said and done, who really cares if you're the best in the world or you make the most money or have the hippest clothes, or if you are fat or skinny or bald or whatever? I knew I was missing something.

That is the moment, I said OK to God. "Here is your shot," I told him, "I am giving you my wrecked body and life. Let's see what you can do with it." Well, to my surprise, God started to clean house. It took the better part of a year, searching and striving to understand and know him just a little. But eventually, I found that giving your life to God has nothing to do with the stiffness, the judgment, the rigidity of the church I had known before.

And it has everything to do with joy, love, grace, forgiveness and power. I was so psyched! People that truly know and love God are those that shine. They aren't the ones that look down their noses at you. They are the ones that love you without limit. They are selfless. They give! They serve. They are full of a joy that is just not normal. They have a confidence and a wisdom that surpass anyone you have ever met. They are different. They are the people that make you wonder what it is they know or have that you don't. Have you figured it out yet? I finally did. It's God. God is the difference in their lives, and now I have him too.

The cool thing is God wants you to know him also. And he waits ever so patiently for you to turn to him. Christ is available to everyone, no matter who you are, no matter what you have done, or what you're are facing. He will change your life. And it's free! That's why they call it the "gift of grace". You can't earn it and you certainly don't deserve it. But God loves each of us so much that he let his son die, so we could know him personally. God only asks you to make yourself available to him, that you choose him. Then, look out! You are in for the ride of your life.

So, whether you accept Christ now, tomorrow, or years from now, I am glad I got to share what God has done with and for me. He is amazing and full of surprises. I often wonder why it took me so long to just let him take the driver's seat. There is no greater, or more challenging, or more fulfilling ride than the one God has set before me. There is certainly no one else I want to be waiting for me as my ride comes to its final turn. Who will be there for you?

Here are four principles that will help guide you in your first steps toward a new life in Christ.

One Love. One Purpose.

Know that God loves you and he created you to know him personally.

Get that through your head first. You know how your dad, or mom, family, or best friend loves you? Well, triple that love a hundred thousand million times and that's how much God loves you. And the other thing is he created us to know him and have a relationship with him. It seems hard to believe that the God of the universe would want to relate to us, especially when we are such jerks or so dumb most of the time. But it's true. He really thinks we are something special.

He says it in the Bible lots of times, but here are a few examples.

About God's love for us. "God so loved the world, that he gave his only begotten son that whoever believes in him should not perish, but have eternal life" (John 3:16).

About God's plan. " . . . I have come that they may have life, and have it to the full" (John 10:10).

But, there is something that gets in the way of knowing God personally. What is it that keeps us from experiencing his love and grace?

We all fall way, way short.

We are separated from God because we are sinful, so we cannot know him personally or experience his love.

We were originally created to intimately know and hang out with God, but because we are so stubborn about doing things our way and want to follow our own desires, we choose ourselves over God. This choice is evident either outwardly and defiantly by words and/or actions or by remaining indifferent or passive to God's call on our lives. This is what God calls sin.

You see, when dealing with God, you are either in or you're out. There is no "kind of" or "a little bit" when dealing with God. And when you don't follow him or give your life completely to him, you are separate and apart from his presence. We all fall into this category until we make a change.

Here's what God says about it in the Bible:

We are sinful and all fall short of God's holiness and perfection. "All have sinned and fall short of the glory of God" (Romans 3:23).

We are separated from God. "The wages of sin is death" [spiritual separation from God] (Romans 6:23).

God is simply saying that he is perfect and blameless and we are not. When we choose ourselves, we are spiritually dead and lost and full of sin. There is a huge chasm between God and his perfection and us and our imperfection. Picture yourself standing on one side of the Grand Canyon and God on the other. We cannot reach him through our efforts or by trying to be good, because nothing can bring us closer to God—except God himself.

The Gift

Jesus Christ is God's only provision for our sin.

Because we can't cross the "Grand Canyon" of sin on our own to meet him, God sent his son to be the bridge from him to us. A long time ago, God sent Jesus to die in our place so we can know him and hang out with him forever. Jesus Christ is God's son and he came to earth to pay the penalty of wrongdoing in our stead.

It's as if each of us were sitting in a jail cell awaiting our day in the gas chamber to pay the cost of all the wrong we have done. Then, God comes to each of our jail cells, and says, "Here. My son will take your place. You are the one who deserves to die, as you are the one who has sinned, but you have been pardoned. Why? Because I love you. I love you so much, I am sending my son who has done nothing and is blameless and perfect, and he will take your place." And then, Jesus willingly dies for you. Jesus is killed. And you are free.

By God's design, you are able to know him only through Christ's paying the penalty (sacrifice) for you. There is only one way to know God and that is through his son, Christ Jesus.

In the Bible it says this:

Christ died in our place. "God demonstrated his own love toward us, in that while we are yet sinners, Christ died for us" (Romans 5:8).

He rose from the dead. "Christ died for our sins . . . he was buried . . . he was raised on the third day, according to the Scriptures . . . he appeared to Peter, then to the twelve. After that he appeared to more than five hundred . . ." (1 Corinthians15:3-6).

He is the only way to God. "Jesus said to him, 'I am the way, the truth, and the life; no one comes to the father, but through me' " (John 14:6).

OK, so Jesus died in our place, rose up, and appeared to the world alive and resurrected from death. It isn't enough just to know and believe that. You must do something. You must act. You must invite him to change your life and to live inside your heart.

By Invitation Only

We must individually receive Christ as Savior and Lord; then we can know God personally and experience his love.

We can only receive Christ through faith and by personal invitation. It takes faith to ask God into your heart and with this faith, you must ask Christ to be that bridge to God, to be your Savior. You must personally choose Christ to be the foundation and center of your life. God will not force himself into our lives or choose for us. We must choose him.

God says the following about receiving Christ:

It is through faith we must receive him. "By grace you have been saved through faith; and that not of yourselves, it is gift of God; not as a result of works, that no one should boast" (Ephesians 2:8,9).

[Christ says] "Behold, I stand at the door and knock; and if any one hears my voice and opens the door, I will come in to him" (Revelation 3:20).

Christ knocks and knocks and knocks. He is tireless. But, he won't come in until you open the door. You have to do it. He will never bust down the door. It is up to you to want to know Christ and when you decide, only then will he come in.

When we receive Christ, we are born again. Read John 3:1-8.

A New Life.

> *It takes only a willing and sincere heart to ask God into your life.*

To become a Christian, you need only say a short prayer (talk with God) to acknowledge the death of Christ in your place and your need for Christ to be at the center of your life. Don't worry about what you say to God, as he is only concerned with your attitude and sincerity. Just talk from your guts and heart.

Or you can read this prayer:

> *Dear God, thanks so much for sending your son to die in my place. I want to know you personally. I want you to change my life. I want you to be the center of who I am. Thank you for forgiving my sins and giving me eternal life with you. Now, take my life and make me who you want me to be, and give me the courage and strength to go where you want me to go. Amen.*

If you prayed this prayer with a sincere heart, Christ is now alive in you and is already beginning a new work in your life. Awesome! Now that you are a Christian and God is in the driver's seat, here are some changes that have occurred whether you realize it yet or not:

- Christ is in your life. (Rev. 3:20, Col. 1:27)

- Your sins are forgiven. (Col. 1:14)

- You are a child of God. (John 1:12)

- You have eternal life. (John 5:24)

- Buckle up! You are on the great adventure for which God created you. (John 10:10; 2 Cor. 5:17; I Thes. 5:18)

Now what?

The key now is to keep searching to know God by talking with him (prayer), reading about Him (in the Bible and other Christian books), going to church, and getting to know other Christians. The more you go to God daily in prayer, read the Bible, obey and trust God in even the tiny things, show and share your life in Christ with others, and allow the God to control and empower you, the more you will experience the incredible gifts and abundance of life with him.

As a helpful reminder, don't rely on your feelings or emotions to see if God is within you. Much of the time, our feelings change and are unreliable. That's where faith comes in: God keeps his promises and he is there if you were sincere in your request to know him. You can trust him to keep his word.

Free Stuff for Guidance

If you'd like more information on knowing God and growing in your relationship with him, or this appendix and book have been helpful to you, please let us know. We not only want to hear your story, but want to send you some free stuff to help you grow as a Christian.

Send your letter to:

Integrated Resources
100 Sunport Lane
Orlando, FL 32809

Principles paraphrased and adapted from a version of *The Four Spiritual Laws* by Bill Bright, *Knowing God Personally,* copyright 1965, 1988, Campus Crusade for Christ, Inc.

Michelle Akers' Achievements / Bio

EDUCATION

1980-84	Shorecrest High School, Seattle, Wa.
1984-89	University of Central Florida Bachelor of Science in Liberal Studies and Health

SOCCER CAREER
United States National Team

1985-present	Starting Striker or CMF
1996	Olympic Gold Medalist
1995	Third Place FIFA World Cup
1991	FIFA World Champion
1991	FIFA World Cup Golden Boot Winner, World Cup leading goal scorer
1991	FIFA Silver Ball Award, Runner-up MVP

All-time leading goal scorer for U.S. Men's and Women's National Team Programs (92 goals in 109 games)

Professional

1990, '92, '94	Tyreso FF Elite Division, Sweden
1992	Canon Shot Award, Sweden's Top Goal Scorer for Men/Women's club leagues

Collegiate

1984-89	University of Central Florida
1984, '85-'89	NCAA 1st Team All-American
1992	Retired Jersey #10
	UCF record holder for career goals/assists
1988	Winner Inaugural Hermann Trophy
1994	Distinguished Alumna Award
1996	The Michelle Akers Award, UCF Alumni Association

Other Honors

1991	U.S. Olympic Committee Athlete of the Year
1990, 1991	U.S. Soccer Federation Female Player of the Year
1990	U.S. Olympic Committee Female Soccer Player of the Year
1985	ESPN Athlete of the Year

EMPLOYMENT
Endorsements

1989-1996	Post To Post International, Inc., Clinician/Technical Director
1993, 1994	Procter & Gamble, Spokesperson/Ambassador for Soccer
1991-1995	Umbro International, Spokesperson/Athlete
1996	Reebok International LTD., Spokesperson/Athlete

Writing Experience

1991   *USA Today*, Guest Columnist
1992-1994   *Soccer International*
1994, 1995 *Sidekicks Magazine*, Columnist
1995-present *Soccer Jr. Magazine*, Columnist

OTHER ASSOCIATED COMMITTEES AND MEMBERSHIPS

1990-1995   U.S. Soccer Federation National Board of Directors
1991-present NSCAA Women's Subcommittee
1992-present Women's Sports Foundation Advisory Board

Advocate for CFIDS Association of America

Founder of The Michelle Akers Fund (with CFIDS Association of America)

Member Northland Community Church

Speaker for Campus Crusade for Christ and Fellowship of Christian Athletes, plus various other organizations and events

For more information about Michelle, check out her homepage on the worldwide web:

www.michelleakers.com

Judith A. Nelson is an associate editor with *Worldwide Challenge* magazine in Orlando, Fla. This is her first book.

Additional Resources

Additional copies of this book as well as other materials from Success Factors* can be ordered from Integrated Resources by calling:

1-800-729-4351

(Visa, Master Card and Discover accepted)

or write to:

Integrated Resources
4307 East Third Street
Bloomington, IN 47401
Fax (812) 339-8389

*An audio cassette telling Michelle Akers' story is available.